...leaf boo

My Healthy Habi

Poison Alert!

My Tips to Avoid Danger Zones at Home

Gina Bellisario

illustrated by **Holli Conger**

Ⓜ MILLBROOK PRESS · MINNEAPOLIS

For Mom, who looks after me —G.B.

For my own little superhero, O.C.,
who always saves my day! —H.C.

Millbrook Press
A division of Lerner Publishing Group, Inc.
241 First Avenue North
Minneapolis, MN 55401 U.S.A.

Website address: www.lernerbooks.com

Main body text set in Slappy Inline 18/28.
Typeface provided by T26.

Library of Congress Cataloging-in-Publication Data

Bellisario, Gina.
    Poison alert! : my tips to avoid danger zones at home / by
Gina Bellisario ; illustrated by Holli Conger.
        p.   cm. — (Cloverleaf books™—My healthy habits)
    Includes index.
    ISBN 978–1–4677–1353–5 (lib. bdg. : alk. paper)
    ISBN 978–1–4677–2532–3 (eBook)
    1. Poisons—Safety measures—Juvenile literature.
2. Accidental poisoning—Juvenile literature. 3. Toxicology—
Juvenile literature. I. Conger, Holli, illustrator. II. Title.
RA1214.B45 2014
615.9'05—dc23   2013024308

Manufactured in the United States of America
1 – BP – 12/31/13

TABLE OF CONTENTS

Chapter One

Mega Mouth

Hi! I'm Matthew. You can call me Mighty Matthew.
I'm playing superheroes with my little brother, Owen.
He's my sidekick, Mega Mouth.

Uh-oh. Mega Mouth is too close to Nana's medicine. Mighty Matthew to the rescue!

Sometimes Owen tries to taste things that aren't food.
Today it's Nana's medicine and Mom's vitamins.
If Owen swallows them, they could make him sick.

They are called harmful substances.

Medicine helps people stay healthy. But before taking any medicine, check with a grown-up. And never take medicine that isn't yours.

Harmful substances are solids, liquids, or gases that can be bad for our health. Does your home have batteries or perfume? Paint, shampoo, or bug spray? These are harmful substances.

Owen is still learning about what's harmful. So I watch over him. It's a job for Mighty Matthew!

100%
PINK

Many cleaning products are made of poisonous chemicals. Stay safe. Do not touch, taste, or smell a cleaning product.

Chapter Two

Super-Villain Hideouts

Harmful substances are like super villains. They have secret hideouts.

The leaves of some houseplants are poisonous. Eating them can hurt us and our pets. Keep all houseplants up high and out of reach.

Houseplants lurk in the kitchen.

Bleach and detergent wait in the laundry room.

Toilet cleaner hides in the bathroom.

Stand back, Mega Mouth!

Harmful substances hide in the garage too. Gasoline makes Mom's car go. Her car also needs motor oil and other fluids. But they give off fumes. Breathing them can hurt our head, eyes, and nose.

The garage is no place to play.
Mom swoops in to save the day!

The backyard is a BIG hideout.
Dangerous substances can hide in the
grass. Herbicides stop pesky weeds.
Pesticides keep away plant pests.

Touching these substances can make you sick. But you can protect yourself. After playing outside, **wash your hands!**

A-1 Lawn Care

Fertilizer is a type of herbicide. Many fertilizers are made of harmful chemicals. Other fertilizers are made from natural ingredients. They contain safer chemicals. Natural fertilizers are better for animals, Earth, and you!

Chapter Three

Poison Squad

No more playing for Mega Mouth. It's time for his nap. While Owen rests, Mom, Nana, and I play superheroes. We make our home safe.

Call us the Poison Squad!

What if a harmful substance makes someone sick? Get help right away. Call the National Capital Poison Center. The phone number is 1-800-222-1222. You can also dial 9-1-1.

We store cleaning supplies out of reach.

Wood Duster

Glass Cleaner

100% PINE

We lock up medicine and vitamins.

Outside we use homemade herbicides and pesticides.

SOAP

White Vinegar

Cigarettes are another harmful substance. Cigarette smoke hurts our lungs. Alcohol can also be harmful. These substances are not for children.

Owen's nap is over. But I'm not worried.
Mighty Matthew will keep him safe.

Team up with your family. Find ways to protect your health. Be a **health hero** today!

Make a "Green" Cleaner

Not all household cleaners have poisonous chemicals in them. Some cleaners are "green." They are better for the environment. Green cleaners are made from natural ingredients. They keep a house clean. But they're safer to use. (Even so, they should still stay away from your eyes and mouth.) Want your own green cleaner? Make one with a grown-up's help. Here's how:

What you need:
1 cup water
large measuring cup
1 cup distilled white vinegar
empty spray bottle (16 oz. or larger)
marker
paper towels or cleaning rags

1) Pour 1 cup of water into the measuring cup. (Be careful not to use hot water.) Add 1 cup of vinegar to the water.

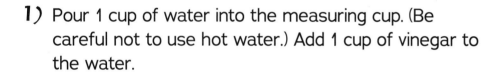

2) Pour the water and vinegar mixture into an empty spray bottle.

3) With a marker, write "Green Cleaner" on the spray bottle. That way, you'll know what's inside.

4) Grab some paper towels or rags and start cleaning! Spray the kitchen counter, and wipe the dirt away. Wash the bathroom floor. Clean doorknobs and handles. By cleaning the "green" way, you'll make your home healthier for your family. And YOU!

GLOSSARY

chemicals: substances that are found in nature or made by science

fluids: liquids

fumes: gases

gases: substances that have no fixed shape, such as air

herbicides: a product used to stop unwanted plants from growing

ingredients: things that make up a mixture

liquids: substances that can flow freely, such as water

9-1-1: a phone number to call during emergencies

pesticides: a product used to stop plant pests

poisonous: harmful

solids: substances that are firm or hard

substances: materials that are solid, liquid, or gas

vitamins: pills that are taken for nutrition

BOOKS

Deboo, Ana. *Safety Around the House.* Chicago: Heinemann Library, 2008.
Read this book to learn about chemicals and other dangers in your home.

Senker, Cath. *Avoiding Harmful Substances.* New York: PowerKids Press, 2008.
This book gives safety tips for taking medicine. And it explains the difference between helpful and harmful drugs.

Spilsbury, Louise. *Harmful Substances.* New York: PowerKids Press, 2012.
This book has photos of harmful substances. It also suggests ways to protect yourself at home and in your yard.

WEBSITES

Mighty Kids Media
http://www.dangerrangers.com/kids_safety_topic.php?id=41
Meet the Danger Rangers and learn poison prevention tips. You can also play games and watch videos about harmful substances.

National Capital Poison Center
http://www.poison.org/prevent/elementary.asp
Watch a poison adventure video from the National Capital Poison Center. Or play some poison adventure games.

U.S. Environmental Protection Agency
http://www.epa.gov/pesticides/kids/index.htm
Visit this site to learn about chemicals used at home. Find out how to keep your backyard free of pesticides too.

LERNER SOURCE
Expand learning beyond the printed book. Download free, complementary educational resources for this book from our website, www.lerneresource.com.